STANDARDS & GEMS

Arranged by Chad Johnson

2	Autumn Leaves
4	Cheek to Cheek
6	Easy to Love
8	Fly Me to the Moon
10	I Only Have Eyes for You
12	It Had to Be You
14	Laura
16	Mack the Knife
18	My Funny Valentine
20	Theme from "New York, New York"
22	Over the Rainbow
24	Satin Doll
26	Some Day My Prince Will Come
28	Summertime
30	The Way You Look Tonight
32	**Notes from the Arranger & Fretboard Charts**

ISBN 978-1-4768-2302-7

HAL•LEONARD®
CORPORATION
7777 W. BLUEMOUND RD. P.O. BOX 13819 MILWAUKEE, WI 53213

Visit Hal Leonard Online at
www.halleonard.com

Autumn Leaves

English lyric by Johnny Mercer
French lyric by Jacques Prevert
Music by Joseph Kosma

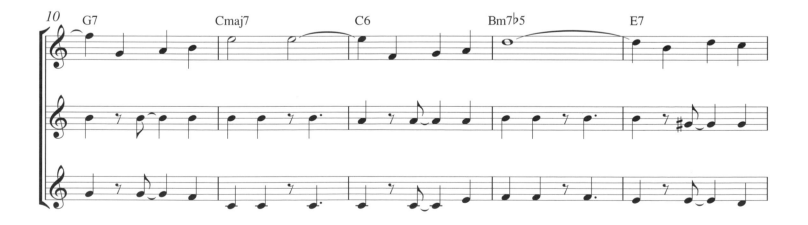

B

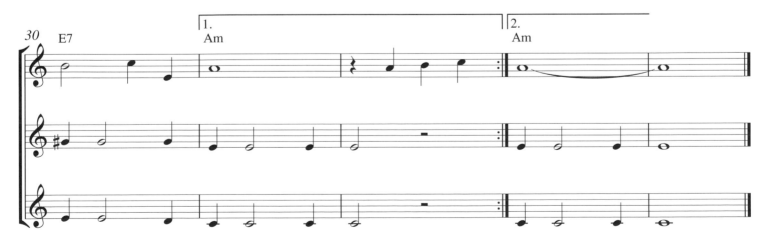

Cheek to Cheek

from the RKO Radio Motion Picture TOP HAT

Words and Music by Irving Berlin

Easy to Love
(You'd Be So Easy to Love)
from BORN TO DANCE

Words and Music by Cole Porter

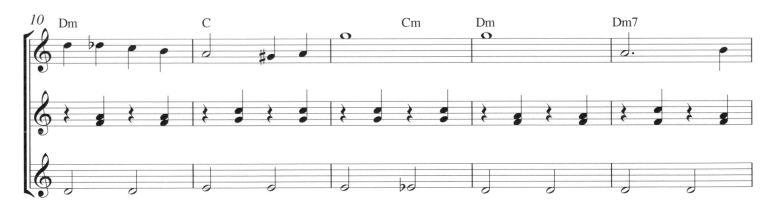

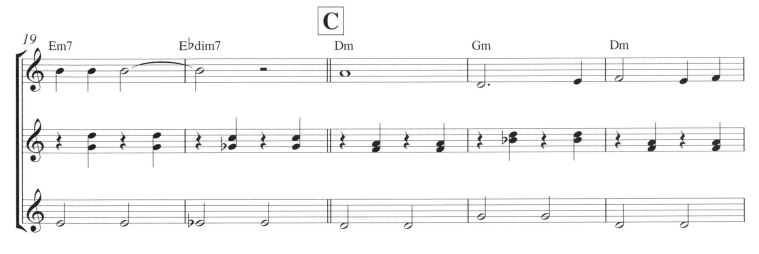

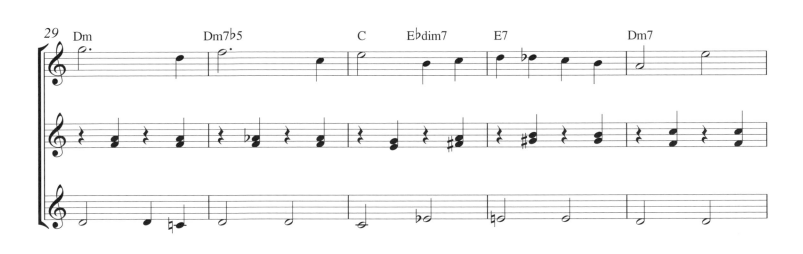

Fly Me to the Moon
(In Other Words)

Words and Music by Bart Howard

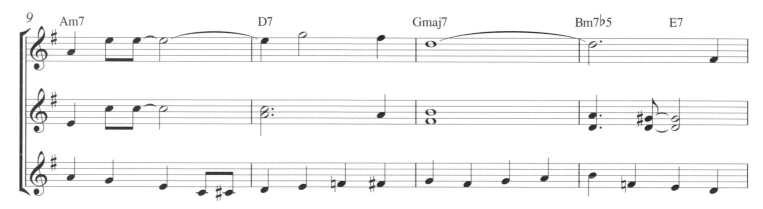

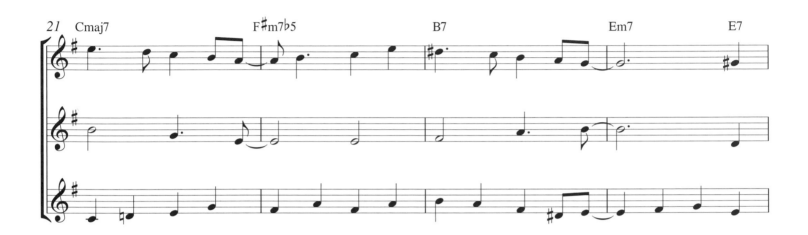

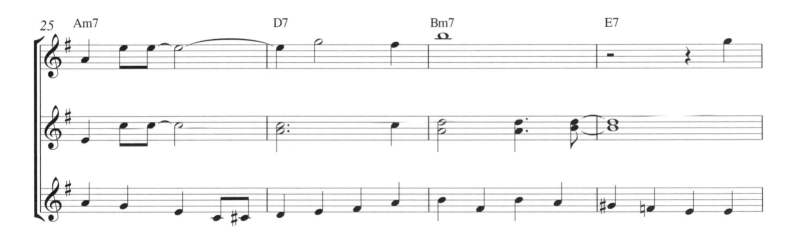

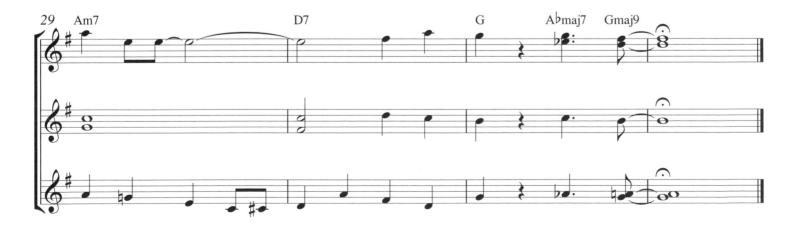

I Only Have Eyes for You

Words by Al Dubin
Music by Harry Warren

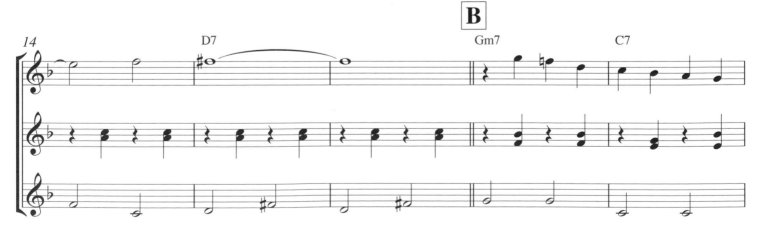

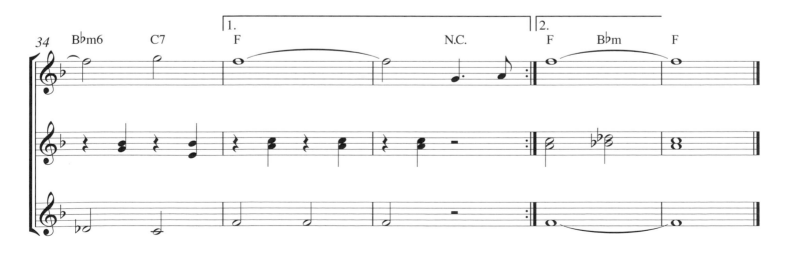

It Had to Be You

Words by Gus Kahn
Music by Isham Jones

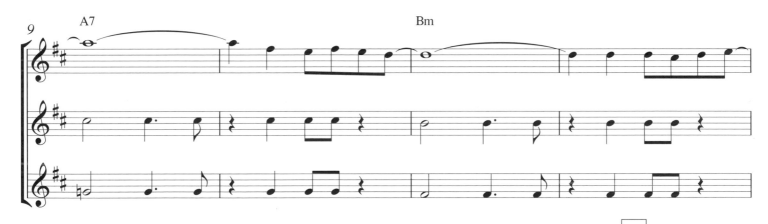

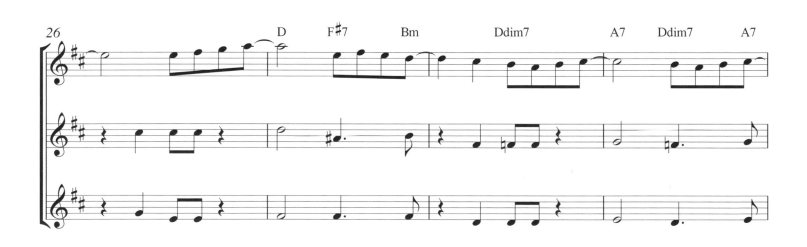

Laura

Lyrics by Johnny Mercer
Music by David Raksin

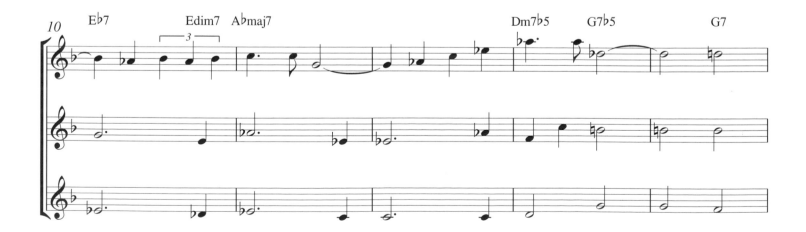

B

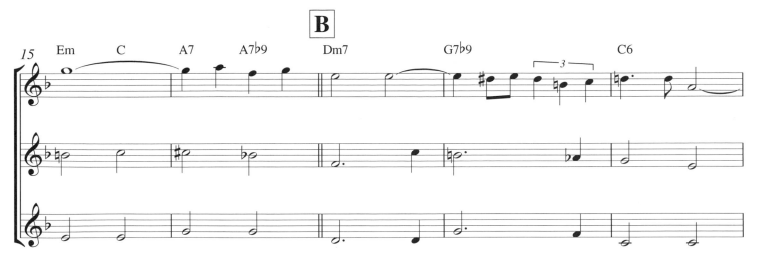

Mack the Knife
from THE THREEPENNY OPERA

English Words by Marc Blitzstein
Original German Words by Bert Brecht
Music by Kurt Weill

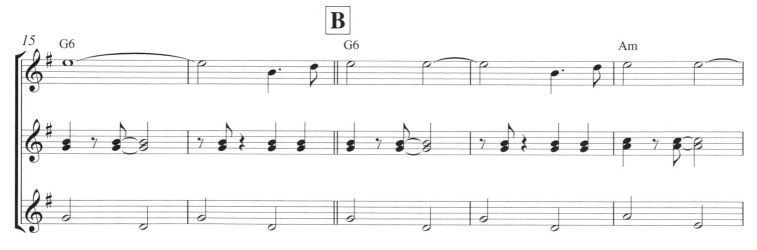

My Funny Valentine

from BABES IN ARMS

Words by Lorenz Hart
Music by Richard Rodgers

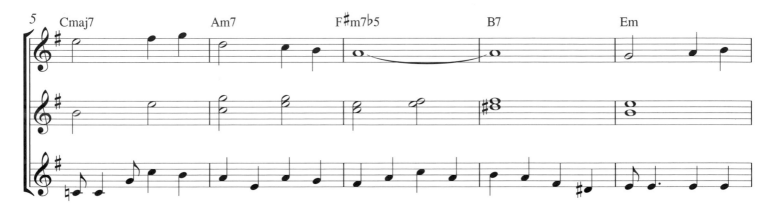

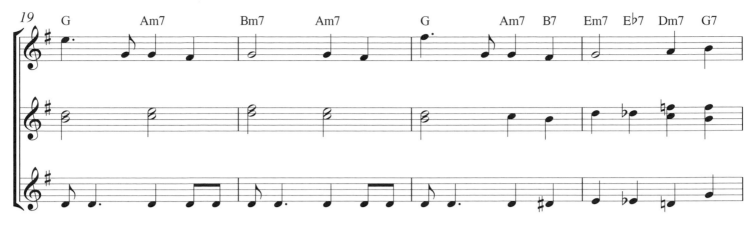

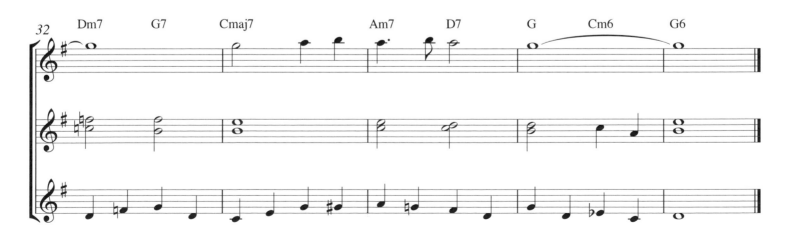

Theme from "New York, New York"

Words by Fred Ebb
Music by John Kander

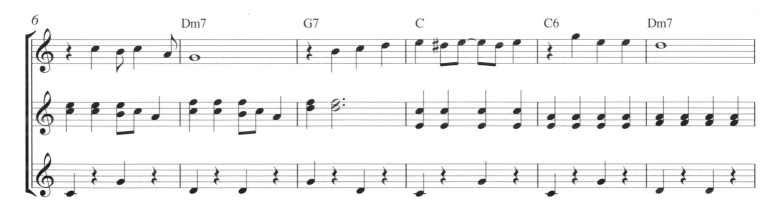

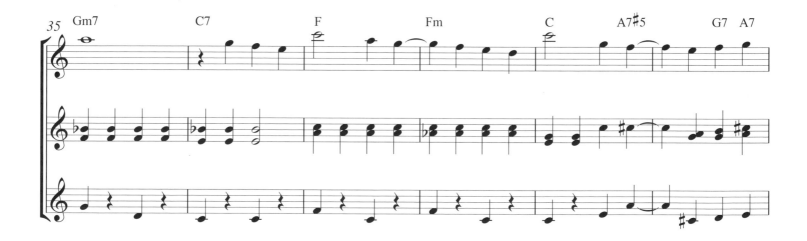

Over the Rainbow

from THE WIZARD OF OZ

Music by Harold Arlen
Lyric by E.Y. "Yip" Harburg

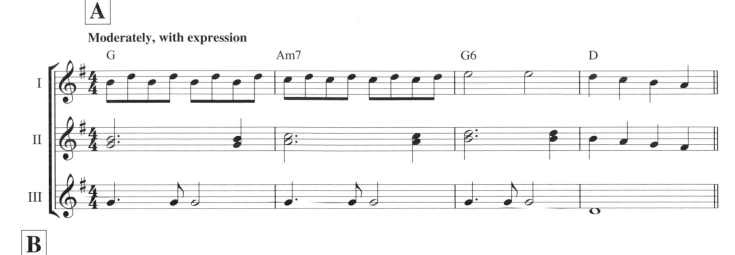

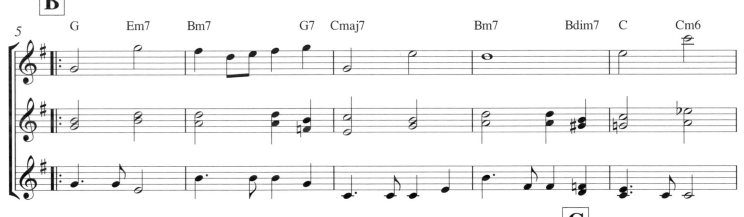

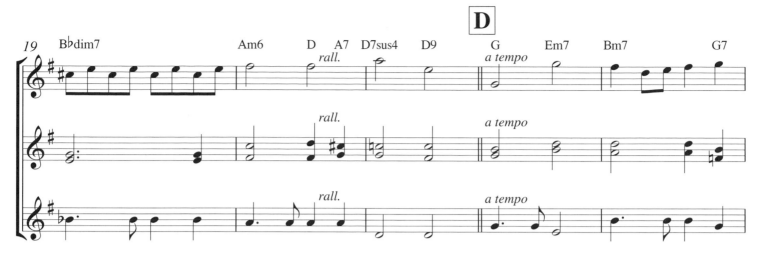

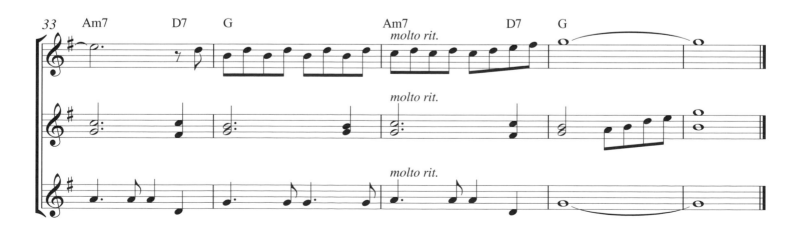

Satin Doll

By Duke Ellington

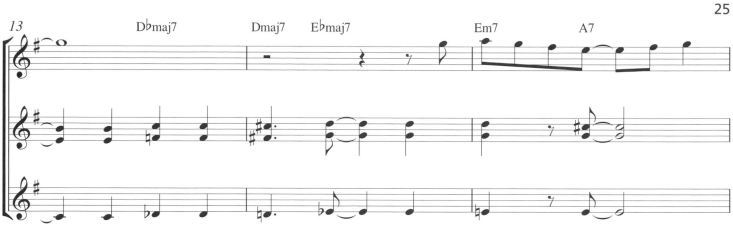

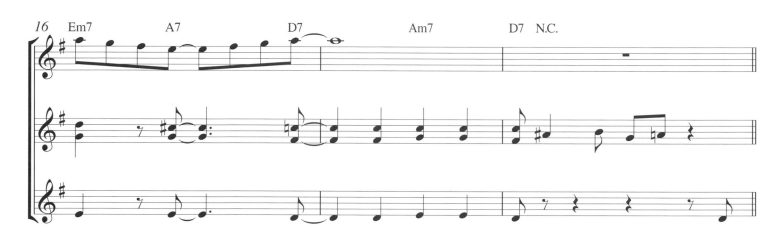

Some Day My Prince Will Come

Words by Larry Morey
Music by Frank Churchill

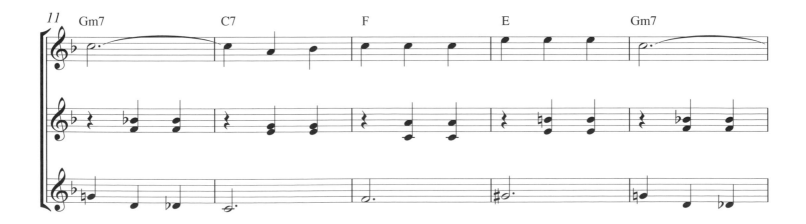

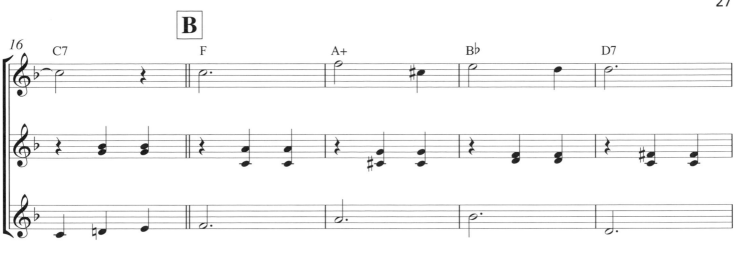

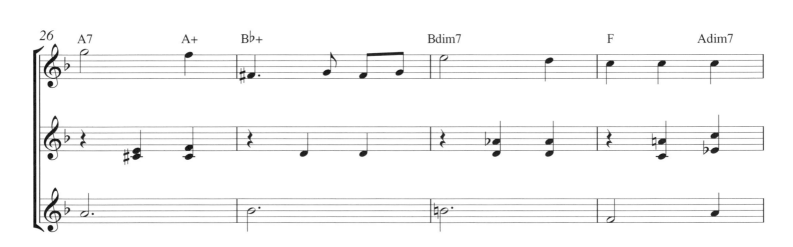

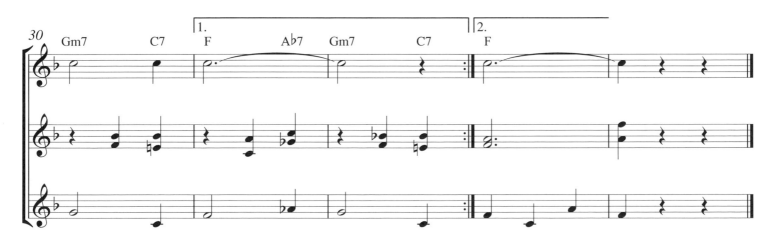

Summertime
from PORGY AND BESS®

Music and Lyrics by George Gershwin, Du Bose and
Dorothy Heyward and Ira Gershwin

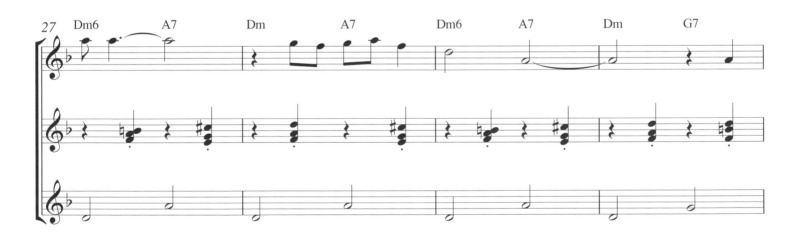

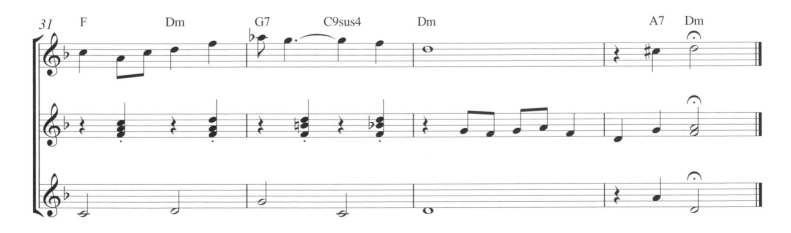

The Way You Look Tonight

from SWING TIME

Words by Dorothy Fields
Music by Jerome Kern

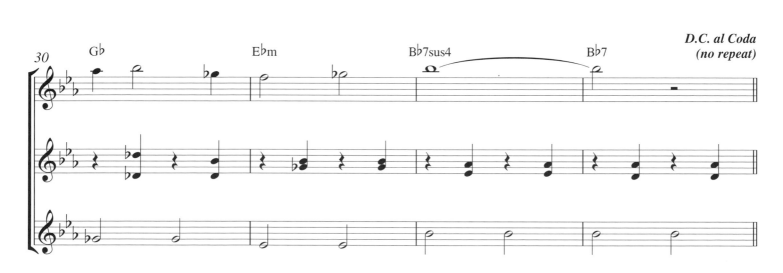

NOTES FROM THE ARRANGER

Arranging for three ukuleles can be challenging because of the instrument's limited range. In standard tuning (G-C-E-A), there is only one octave plus a major sixth between the open C string and fret 12 on the A string. Certain melodies easily span this distance and more, so compromises sometimes had to be made.

Not all ukuleles have the same number of frets. If your uke has fewer than 15 frets, you may need to play certain phrases an octave lower (especially in Part I). Some phrases have already been transposed up or down an octave—this was only done out of necessity and kept to a minimum. A few songs require every inch of available fretboard, but fret 15 on the first string (high C) is the limit, and this is extremely rare.

The three voices will sometimes cross as a result of range limitations. If Part III is considered to be the "bass" line, keep in mind that the lowest available "bass" notes are sometimes on the first string! However, if you own a baritone ukulele, almost all of the notes in Part III could be played an octave lower (except the open C string and C♯ on fret 1), thus providing a more effective bass line.

Despite the above caveats, I believe that the spirit of these songs has been preserved, and I hope you enjoy playing these arrangements as much as I enjoyed creating them. By the way, a fourth ensemble part can be added by strumming along with the chord symbols!

– Chad Johnson

SOPRANO, CONCERT & TENOR FRETBOARD

BARITONE FRETBOARD

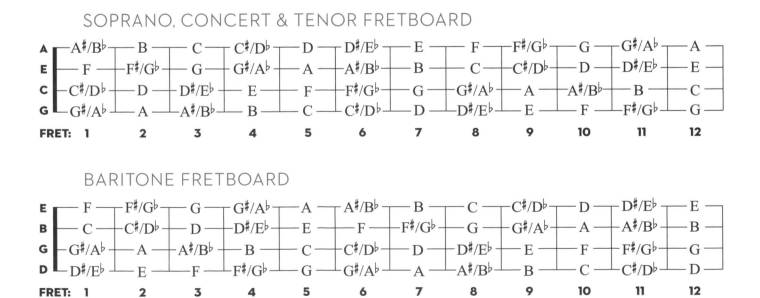